W9-AJO-085

You Are What You Eat

By Sharon Gordon

Consultants
Nanci Vargus, Ed.D.
Primary Multiage Teacher
Decatur Township Schools, Indianapolis, Indiana

Jayne L. Waddell, R.N., M.A., L.P.C.
School Nurse/Health Educator/Lic. Professional Counselor

Children's Press®
A Division of Scholastic Inc.
New York   Toronto   London   Auckland   Sydney
Mexico City   New Delhi   Hong Kong
Danbury, Connecticut

Designer: Herman Adler Design
Photo Researcher: Caroline Anderson
The photo on the cover shows a child eating.

Library of Congress Cataloging-in-Publication Data

Gordon, Sharon.
  You are what you eat / by Sharon Gordon.
      p. cm. — (Rookie read-about health)
Includes index.
Summary: Discusses basic facts about nutrition, the food pyramid, and
the importance of making healthy food choices.
  ISBN 0-516-22573-1 (lib. bdg.)   0-516-26952-6 (pbk.)
  1. Nutrition—Juvenile literature. [1. Nutrition.] I. Title. II. Series.
RA784 .G67 2002
  613.2—dc21

                                    2002005485

What is that noise?

4

Your stomach is growling.
It even hurts a little.
It is telling you to eat
some food—soon!

You need food and drink every day. It is very important to eat the right foods. Eating healthy foods will help you do your best.

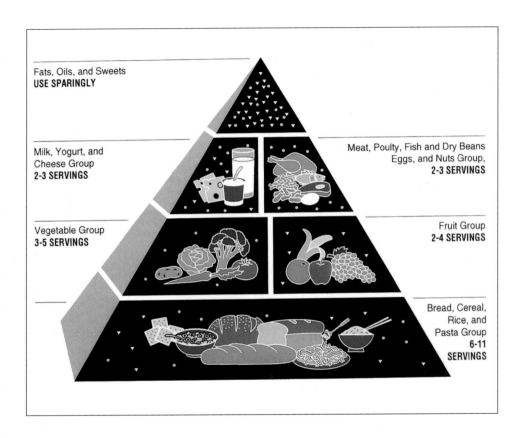

Fats, Oils, and Sweets
USE SPARINGLY

Milk, Yogurt, and
Cheese Group
2-3 SERVINGS

Meat, Poulty, Fish and Dry Beans
Eggs, and Nuts Group,
2-3 SERVINGS

Vegetable Group
3-5 SERVINGS

Fruit Group
2-4 SERVINGS

Bread, Cereal,
Rice, and
Pasta Group
**6-11
SERVINGS**

Try to eat something from each food group every day.

Look at this food pyramid to see how much you should eat from each food group. You should eat the most from the bread, cereal, rice, and pasta group.

You should not eat too much, or too little, of one thing. Each kind of food has something special your body needs to stay healthy.

It is important to make good choices when you eat. Try not to eat too many sweets. You want to save room for foods that are good for your body.

Always start your day
with a good breakfast.
Never go to school with
an empty stomach.

Without breakfast, you will
feel tired. It will be hard
for you to listen and learn.

Try a bowl of cereal.
Add a sliced banana.

Some people like to have eggs for breakfast. How do you like yours cooked?

What will you eat for lunch? This girl is eating a healthy lunch with pasta, vegetables, meat, and milk.

19

20

A sandwich with
lunchmeat and lettuce
is another good choice.

What will you have to drink? Milk is good for your growing bones.

There are many kinds of delicious juices, too. They can give your body vitamins.

23

Do you like to snack
after school? Make it
a healthy snack.

Have something from the
fruit or vegetable groups.

It is time to make dinner.
Try some tossed salad.

Have bread with some soup.

Now that you have finished a healthy meal, a small dessert would be okay.

Words You Know

breakfast

dessert

food pyramid

healthy

milk

pasta

snack

tired

31

Index

About the Author

Sharon Gordon is a writer living in Midland Park, New Jersey. She and her husband have three school-aged children and a spoiled pooch. Together they enjoy visiting the Outer Banks of North Carolina as often as possible.

Photo Credits

Photographs © 2002: Folio, Inc./Tom and Dee Ann McCarthy: 15, 31 bottom right; H. Armstrong Roberts, Inc./L. Fritz: 26; ImageState/Images Colour Library: 12, 30 top right; International Stock Photo/Hal Kern: 24, 31 bottom left; Peter Arnold Inc./Jodi Jacobson: 3, 4, 27, 29; Photo Researchers, NY: 19, 31 top right (Richard Hutchings), 7 (Maximilian Stock Ltd./SPL); Stock Boston: 23, 31 top left (Bob Daemmrich), 14, 20, 30 top left (Lawrence Migdale), 17 (Richard Pasley); Stone/Getty Images/Amy Neunsinger: 16; Superstock, Inc.: 11, 30 bottom right; The Image Bank/Getty Images: cover; USDA: 8, 30 bottom left.